Black Magic

Poems by R.C. Patterson

Kansas City Spartan Press Missouri

Spartan Press
Kansas City, Missouri
spartanpresskc.com

Copyright (c) R.C. Patterson, 2018
First Edition 1 3 5 7 9 10 8 6 4 2
ISBN: 978-1-946642-57-8
LCCN: 2018948311

Design, edits and layout: Jason Ryberg, Jeanette Powers
Cover painting and layout: RC Patterson, Oscar Fernandes
Author photo: RC Patterson
All rights reserved. No part of this publication may be reproduced or transmitted in any form or by any means, electronic or mechanical, including photocopying, recording or by info retrieval system, without prior written permission from the author.

Spartan Press would like to thank Prospero's Books, The Fellowship of N-finite Jest, The Prospero Institute of Disquieted P/o/e/t/i/c/s, Will Leathem, Tom Wayne, Jeanette Powers, j. d. tulloch, Jon Bidwell, Jason Preu, Mark McClane, Tony Hayden and the whole Osage Arts Community.

I want to thank Lovie and Randolph Patterson, Demosthenes "Mike" Hill, Oscar Fernandes, Michelle Patterson and Olivia Patterson.

-RC

CONTENTS

Blood Stained / 1

Magush / 4

I'm Always Tipsy / 7

She Came / 8

Her Tartarus / 9

The Night, the Corner of Arsenal / 10

Trapped in the Margins / 14

Toy Gun / 15

25 to Life / 17

The Boy / 19

The Flower on the Chair / 21

The Rock / 23

What Does It Mean to be a Realist? / 25

Elegy 1 of Erotica Matrix / 26

Trapped Like Mice / 27

Reaching for the Sky / 28

We Rock the Spot / 30

The Colony / 32

Run Don't Look Back Just Run / 34

Having This Gift is Like Having a Gun / 38

Phone Rings / 40

Disagreements Among Friends / 43

Physicians and Philologists / 45

Talking to My Dad / 46

$5.00 is too much for one noodle. / 50

Somnambulist / 52

Stygian Street / 53

Brand Nubian / 56

Black Magic

To my loving mother, Lovie Patterson

Blood Stained

I woke up in the humid sweltering South.
Where you can be a farmer or a laborer.
Where the overseer can get it.
Where uncle only got a year,
because they couldn't prove it.

They couldn't prove that blood was on my hands
because my style is bloodstains
on hands I don't see.
Hands chopped off in the Congo.
Hands that are tools,
tools like my father used during the war,
the war for his family after a prick threatened to
kill his family with no regrets.
The prick challenged the black Rambo.
Sambo chain link hits was the response across
the face of that prick.
Daddy did some time.
Thoughts heavy,
Jungle warfare.
In held an orange code.
Wandered forlorn to four kids.
Ten-hour working days.
A Vietnam veteran Oliver Twist
working to earn that porridge.

A smoker, a drinker, transitioned to a preacher.
Worked thirty years, married to a teacher.
Buried his father.
Thoughts abought Viet Cong slaughters,
Vietnamese bodies piled in attrition stacks,
like pancakes.
Warehoused G.I. bodies,
moving them like shipping crates.

I woke up in the humid sweltering South.
Where you can only be a farmer or a laborer.
Where the overseer can get it.
Where uncle only got a year,
because they couldn't prove it.

They say grandfather escaped slavery
by running to a sheltered grotto,
a cave.
For a decade black Zarathustra
lived off milk and honey.
For ten years
great grandfather hid as a runaway.
Grandmother moved from being a serf
to a matriarch.
She carried a revolver,
pistol whipping heads spinning like
bullet chambers across the face
of her daughter's husband.

He used to beat her.
Swing his hands
like a baseball bat across her face.
Threading her cheek with blood and hand prints.
Until his face became a textile grandmother
sewed so many knots in his head you could hitch
a trailer to them and drive
his docile ass to St. Louis.
Where her granddaughter
can escape Jim Crow's nest.
Migrating, fleeing to a dying city.

Magush

I give you that Old Persian magush.
A member of the priestly class.
A Chaldean Negro,
selling salsa to Latins
since my salad days when
Latins ran the Southern European salt trade.
Paid soldiers a salary of salt.

Her scowl was bitter as salty tears I cause
because I forgot her birthday.
She was angry as a bear gnawing its leg off,
because it's trapped in a bear trap.
I came late as my mother when she had me.
I had candy and Brandy,
but she was pissed as my pants
after a night of debauchery
She wanted an axe sent at me.

I said,

I'm sorry,

like a fireman witnessing a conflagration
they could have stopped.

She said,
I tried to call you.

Crying like the Niagara during a monsoon.
Hit her with some black magic.
Hugged her like skin hugs muscle,
like a black hole hugs light,
like old school wannabes hold on to 90s rap.
She forgave me.

Niggers wonder where I get the black magic.
The power to keep going.
The power to re-define the tragic.

My cousin found his momma sleeping,
dreaming with Jesus.
Beneath cold sheets,
on the floor.
He tried lifting her up,
but she was higher than the space station.
He was melancholic
until I him hit with the black magic.
Now he accepted death as another journey
through time and memory.

The ancestor's crest is a black magic symphony.
You see I get the black magic
from the Old Persian magush.
This golden jade was carefully crafted by
an enslaved Songhia jeweler in a Muslim majority
province in western China.

Rising to a member of the priestly class.
A Chaldean Negro
selling salsa to Latins since my salad days
I've been the blackest magician.

I'm Always Tipsy

I'm always tipsy,
sweet like coleslaw until I start tripping.
Fuck tipping!
The waiter asked me for the check
I said *stop acting flippant*.

I took his check because I'd rather pay
misdemeanor's fine, like Casey Anthony.
She got the kids in the divorce.
She left me because of fucking felony.

Felony had more to offer.
Still a prison,
but a prison with a corner office.

I'm just glad
I got teach my son semantics, how to understand
that when proposition speaks
she means whatever the fuck she says.

I'm like a condiment, how I relish the times
in her buns.
After a modest proposal
I swiftly got in a position
where proposition
could back up my every decision.
This is how I'm living.

She Came

She's coming, she's cunning.
She likes you, your risk taking excites her;
she likes the sunlight,
she likes the nighttime.
The eternal nighttime.

Oh, she's coming, she's cunning.
Met her at night.
She crept into bed.

Oooh, she's cumming.
Her love feels like slow heart beats
in quick succession.
She grips my arm.

Her sex is paralyzing.

Her love feels like cold toes grasping warm air.
Her love feels like everything stopped.
In a moment blood pulses stop.
In a moment all thought stops.

She came.

Her Tartarus

Incarcerated in her Tartarus,
charred and naked.
Stripped of my mark, stained with
feelings in the sea off her dark embankment.

Feelings of debt.
Eternally I owe you.
You're my navigator,
speaking in compass.

I burned in her mantle.
A love that pulled me from my cave,
where flames whip shadow slaves
who rattle chains until you,
on a saddle, came
to know me
and show me truth.

Eternally I owe you.
You're my navigator,
I've been for searching you.

The Night, the Corner of Arsenal

In the low temperature, under October skies,
I felt my soul centered. I was always wondering where
my mind was. It was on thoughts of her. I thought of
her in *ought* patterns. We ought, should. If I had my
way, we would be committed. That day she texted me.
She had a smooth way of hexing me. I always gave her
the best of me, she said,

Meet me at my place.

My face lit up. Even if I was feeling lethargic as a
carcass, buried up to the head, I still would have gone.
Drove to her apartment. Entered her dwelling place.
Released all the stress of the day. I forgot about my
last heart break the heart ache I used to partake in
was gone.

We went to Rosalita's, sat in a booth, had some
margaritas. She had a Cuban, I had burrito. She told
me about her day. The United Way was giving her
and her coworkers preparedness training just in case
Black Mad Max came armed. Downtown was
concerned about niggas coming. Fearing nigger
attacks, like they were ISIS.

We moved to the bar to hear the verdict. Third person
to these events we heard it and we saw it. Cop car flipped
and burned. Left Rosalita's, went back to her place.
Watched Ferguson burn on her laptop. Car lots, black
business. Self-destruction, suicidal eruptions reminds me
of my death wish, and my absolution after I left that shit.

On her PC we watched protesters gather at Arsenal
and South Grand. With an arsenal of peaceful demands.
Civilians disobedient, ingredients beginning to bake into
crowds on the screen we wanted to see it. Spectators to
an anarchist's dream.

We have no reason to be down there, but I want to go,
she said.

*Most of the people down there have no business down
there, so let's go.*

So we left.

It was happening up the street. The bondsman
grappling with his lordship. Protesters lit up standing in
darkness we wanted to see the spectacle we walked up
there, swiftly, to a meter a little fearful, but eager wanted
to see a car wreck, city wreck. We walked by broken
windows, doors boarded up, glass littered streets.
Shop owners forced to clean their store fronts.

Beneath the night sky an owner glared at me with spite.
Wanting to smite me, I saw hate rising, emanating through
the tenebrous pores on his scowling face, or maybe just
pissed about his broke shit and he had to stay up all night.

Couple of police trucks, armored vehicles. A man stole
a crossbow bow across the street illegal activities criminal
nativities spawned all over.

So many people came down to protest, but they gave up,
or maybe they were done, or maybe they were infiltrated
to that degree with looters. guerrilla soldiers of opportunity.

A crowd formed around the Qdoba. It was boarded up, about to be open and smoking. Now it's almost like stereotypes of monkey daguerreotypes are confirmed. In front of us some Negroes were sitting down one masked kid said,

Don't stand behind us!

So we walked around the building. Niggers about to do something grimy.

Across the street, we saw cops marching down in phalanx to stamp out darkies and hippies who didn't leave.

The modern King Macedon came to stamp out the Greco free speech. They stopped, kneeled down to pray to beseech white Christ for safety.

I stood across the street with my lover's hand across from the horror of the other, the police man. Choppers hovered over officers praying, preparing to release the dam.

Almost walked up to get a picture, decided against it, took one from the distance. She, my angel, got closer and got a better picture.

When the cops started to march towards those looting the Qdoba. A battalion of armored vehicles was on South Grand moving north while the phalanx, the city's soldiers, running off donuts and Folgers, were marching south, hunting. They surrounded those who didn't run away. Those who were actually there to protest the innocent were drowned in the noxious spray.

I heard five pops at once. Next to me, a cannister of tear gas exploded. We ran away. Ran with the crowd.

People in the crowd were coughing. Streets were blocked off, good thing we were walking. When we made it back, we turned on the news. the man who stole the crossbow was caught, we also saw the only protester that was left in the mist of tear gas.

Trapped in the Margins

At the margins dark kids run
until it's no way out of the auto-de-fé.

At the margins dark kids make art lives
far from galleries.
But these buildings are galleries.
Alley ways immersed in color, in valleys,
days cursed smothered in a love for media.
Music sirens call hovering over violence.

Neighbors stay silent, some lying,
others run in a flight and precious justice
becomes a blight.

A blame game that furthers the powerful
and aids no one,
because all become implicit cowards beneath
the purple sky

Beneath the purple sky
I bequeath unseen minds as I hurdle mines.
The mist surrounds me with sounds of
astounding screams touching my face.
I run until there is no way out of the auto-de-fé.

Toy Gun

I was seven, playing with maple tree branches in the front yard. The front yard was surrounded by a rusted silver gate. At the end of the yard there was a mix of corkwood shrubs and evergreen bushes. Closer to the house there was a large sycamore and an over-grown maple tree. The yard was as spacious as the distances between places I used to go to in my imagination, and I used to pretend to hunt birds while mom made dinner.

I used to play outside underneath the azureous sea of sky that provided the perfect cerulean frame to the corn-colored sun. I would hunt birds with a modified dart gun that shot AA batteries. But the birds always escaped my gigantic slow-moving battery bullets.

In the basement I would snipe at old soda cans. I was a Mafia assassin, killing aluminum can bosses with a nerf gun I herded up soldiers and action figures. I'd squeeze the plastic trigger with the accuracy of a Navy Seal, because I was a Navy Seal sniper, hyper as a pyromaniac with a can of gasoline and a lighter. I had had no friends except the ones I invented, the personas I put on to escape my listless existence of school, kids who didn't want to play with me, and homework that I did quite poorly. However, my toy guns, and eventually video games, cardboard crossbows and rectangular Lego battleships gave me a place where I served a purpose.

I was a Navy Seal.

This is why I felt some solidarity with Tamir Rice. Because kids play with toy guns, some kids play with guns outside when it's 25 degrees with clouds like tapeworms outstretched and ashen with dead sienna arms reaching for the indigo skies that are hidden behind the gray.

Some kids use orange capped pistols to take out imaginary targets, running like Navy Seals, ducking behind hazel trees until a phone rings. A woman spies a child playing with a pistol from her window.

She has just called 911, the operator hung up before she could say

I think it's a juvenile!

Two cops jaunted to the scene to see who they perceived to be a black man waving a pistol, sitting at a picnic table. If they had only known that he was a Navy Seal then maybe they would have thanked him for finding bin Laden kicking over his life support equipment, then saying

This is for America!

Then plugging two copper cone bullets in his head in the most gangsta way possible, then maybe they wouldn't have shot him, a kid playing pretend before he went home.

25 to Life

Last night
I dreamed about the last family reunion.
The homemade family history documentary.
Images of my mother,
my aunts, my cousins
streamed across the screen,
but my eye stopped
at the image of my brother.

Started crying
like when I was at my uncle RC's funeral.

Fighting to hold back tears
when the video came to the part
where my brother was playing
with the three-year-old me.

He was playing with my cap,
putting it on and off my head
like the parole board was playing with his time.
Dangling it like a treat,
flipping it in the air,
hiding it behind them
and then lying to your face about hiding it.

Putting a baseball cap on and off my head.

This caused the three-year-old me to grin
and giggle involuntarily
with the corners of my mouth
nearly penned to my ears
as my little hands grabbed at my cap
attempting to prevent it from being removed.

I couldn't stop the tears coming from my eyes.

Years ago I asked my momma,

How long is his sentence?

She said, *25 to life!*

Big brother was arrested
for murder by a warrior cop.

The Boy

The boy was set upon by wolves.
Horned wolves with sharp words
and flaming hooves.

Ambulating nightly.
Bare feet suffer wear and tear.
Skin tearing shards of rubble
on shattered concrete.

Caliginous trees
draped in emerald
weep the morning dew.

The boy sips whisky
after licking the teary clear nectar.

Ambulating nightly.
Bare feet get cut up.
The boy was tired.
The boy sits down on an out cropping.

The geography consisted
of a geology of a bloody
incarnadine rock
jetting out into the red dawn.

The boy fell asleep,
but only to dream about wolves.
Horned wolves with sharp words
and flaming hooves.

Shades of a periwinkle sky seemed to float
like drift wood.
A background for the wolves.

The wolves wanted his mouth.
The wolves didn't want him to speak.
They needed to keep him from crying out.

After cutting the boy's throat
the wolves viewed his vocal cords
looking like a series of wires in sanguine paint.

They removed his mouth
and buried his body in the dream world.

The Flower on the Chair

So I remember a slate drape on the horizon. Smoky clouds wrapping the sky like God was saving that blue soup for later. But it was as early as a premature baby.

My big cousin Brian was taking me and his little brother to preschool. I remember a big room full of chairs. A beautiful brilliant brown girl with flowing black hair. She was like waking up in an opium addict's pipe dream of rivers and lush forested valleys singing of cherry colored roses.

For my first love I had a flower. A fake rose red as a sanguine cherry sour on a plastic stick, but love knows not of money. Love literally meant doing something for nothing.

In a room as large as the great opera halls to a 4-year-old with green, yellow, orange and red seats. I sat next to her and offered her the rose red as the heart beating in my chest.

I gutted myself, like an Aztec priest performing hara-kiri. Arteries and veins poured like pus flowing out of an abscess. The pain was as unbearable as scratching my chest with rusted razor blades. My screams were filtered by my need to not scare her away. So anything I said came out in a low tone. Presenting the sanguine cherry flower to her I said,

Here...

I didn't see it then, but she was scared.
Scared of the blood.
Scared of my intense 4-year-old passion.

She took the rose, got up,
then left the rose on the chair.

The Rock

My little cousin and niece used to be snakes slithering into my basement room. Cold blooded little heathens sneaking in my drawers finding, chocolate, sugar coated candies, condom wrappers and video games.

I used to play a game called Soul-Blade. With multiple characters including a new age Nibelung's song sung by Siegfried. Siegfried had conquered the English language to a ridiculous degree, especially for a Medieval German. After every victory he used to say,

I will not rest until I have vengeance for my father!

Never realizing that he killed his father. In his suit of argentite armor covering his body in an Achilles fashion he held a sword as long as two tall men.

He would hack at characters like Taki who would effortlessly dodge Siegfried's blade strikes like some ninja fly, or a circus acrobat with a blade short and sharp as Joe Pesci. She was dressed in attire so skin tight that I'm convinced it was painted on her.

One day my cousin snuck in my room and found my escape. My escape to stadiums in castles on plateaus of granite where I can actually succeed after a day of working on one Algebra 1 question only to get it wrong and never know why. But when I was in that stadium I knew why I lost every battle and I learned from every mistake.

She broke it in half, she broke my ship that sailed through the gates of the land of Soul-Blade like a saltine cracker you crumble before you put it in a hot cup of soup. She crumbled my escape into the piping hot cup of my rage.

She was playing outside near the avocado skinned apricot tree. The sky was as gray as snow in the shadows. Grey as the rock I took up the tree. Climbing through yellow, red and incarnadine raw apricots hanging like Christmas ornaments. I was going to drop the rock as a warning.

Clutching it loosely, it started to slip as if it were greased up. I was several feet above my cousin. She looks up as the rock meets her forehead.

What Does It Mean to be a Realist?

What does it mean to be a realist?
It means that happiness exists.
Happiness is as real as numbers drifting like fall
foliage creating a collage painting the canvas of my
imagination, because I see love in the faces of people
who fly through life like biplanes.
Nothing is more beautiful than a positive attitude.
An attitude as genuine as my niece when she says

I love you uncle, look what I got you for your birthday.

As she holds a notebook with several strips of paper
haphazardly glued to the cover.
I refuse to tell her that it's not my birthday.
But this is that honesty that I seek to be like.
Honesty is also real.
Love is real.
This is what it means to be a realist.

Elegy 1 of Erotica Matrix

Here's where I have planted my garden
whose golden fruits are products of
noumenal experiences in the fifth
dimension. A damsel with dementia
weeps parabolas bleeding from
Polonius, stabbed with polonium
Spears.
Apollo must be balanced!
This is why I left the Matrix
with Morpheus.
The Dionysian
machine rivers wake me up from hypnosis.

Trees are pikes impaling
the earth draining her,
like leeches on a lake of blood.
Clouds are gray canvases
I painted with my eyes.
I painted the green,
but it's winter
The damsel with dementia
followed me.
Now I feel my two-ness.
Split like a pizza.
Dinner for Apollo
and the Dionysian.

Trapped Like Mice

Trapped like mice in high towers.
Invisible red lines keep me from food.
He keeps me from her.
Kept from bread crumbs.
Cut off from love.

Trapped like mice in high towers.
Just waiting to starve, to end this living.
Cut off from friends.
No company in this prison.
Just waiting to starve, alone, so hungry.
Why am I still trapped, you won, you don't need me!

Trapped like mice in high towers.
Red lines get trampled.
Burned up and shattered.
Pushed to revolt, can't keep us from shit.
Pushed to assault these red lines and gatekeepers.
I am free, you lost, I can finally see her!

But she found me beneath the rubble of towers.
Cut off from love, her love grew sour.
Kept from bread crumbs.
Her children starved trapped like mice in high towers.

Reaching for the Sky

The night was a periwinkle sea urchin purple. I had just arrived home, about to enter the front gate of my house when I witnessed black jeeps parking behind me. Several officers, in plain clothes and bullet proof vests, exited the jeeps. An officer, who was cautiously looking at me announced,

There had been a shooting, a witness said it was a grey sedan.

At the time, I drove a silver mercury Grand Marquis. Called it the U-boat, because it was enormous. It was big enough to sink into the minds of police officers who pulled me over repeatedly. It was big enough to sink into the minds of these undercover officers searching for a suspect.

As soon as I saw the undercover police gripping pistol handles I raised my hands to God, reaching for the Lord's protection. One undercover officer slowly crept up to me and asked for my license. I told him,

It's in my back pocket,

because I refused to reach.

This was well before Mike Brown.

Police barely search my car. They merely glanced. They didn't find a gun. I know, because I was watching them. It was as if I had eyes that could zoom like a camera.

My eye zoomed in on one officer who opened my trunk, lifted some paper then closed it.

I wondered if I would go to prison, falsely accused with a murder charge, like my brother.

My arms started getting tired, they started to waver, shaking like a mild San Andreas earthquake.

Then one of the officers got a call. Apparently the vehicle was a white jeep. So they left.

We Rock the Spot

We rock the spot.
We got the pots for cooking
eggs, sausage and bacon.
I told my kids respect this, stop draining
the grease from the pan, drink it.
Little stinkers, you was almost aborted
we don't respect you wanna be Peter Singers.
I got more cash to waste, bet
I got more kids in laundry bins
than Genghis Khan got across the whole
central Asian steppe.

We rock the spot,
we got the pots for cooking,
What you think we making.
I told my kids respect this,
stop taking food off my plate then
Throwing that shit in my face.
Tangent
I'm the greatest,
so great I made Muhammad Ali shake.
My pants will catch fire in ether
because I'm hotter
than ghost pepper infused tater tots
I'm so prolific you thought

you was witnessing a Trump mouth diarrhea
I spit millions,
the Missouri Lottery, son
but back to the story
MTV couldn't afford me
so I got a show on NBC.

We rock the spot.
We got the pots for cooking
eggs, sausage and bacon
I told you to respect this,
stop hating
I get drunk with a lot of college students.
None of them is graduating
and they know it, stupids
I gots two scripts, one for my people
and one for these police.
I chew nipples like tobacco.
Then I attack android note pad.
Yo! I'm the truth, off top.

We rocked the spot.

The Colony

Wealthy religious right run All the State.
Draining resources leaving me dehydrated
because I drink the dusty blood of the so called
great men. I rehydrate off the teat of mother
Africa milking wisdom from slain empires.

Mother Africa gives!

Europe takes from American colonies on
dusty roads, smugglers, thieves,
early American hustlers
live under British restrictions.
No rights, no time to feel sorry,
so they revolt.
They empty ships full of tea,
representations of colonial oppression.

This is after years of oppression,
soldiers shooting civilians.
Bullets hit you in the heart,
making you willing to kill.

Sitting in that apartment,
next to the glock.
Got a headache,
the room is tenebrous.

Cops barge in.
You point the pistol
because they ain't announce shit.
Folks trapped in the colony.

In an instant the colonialists took away
the second amendment.
Bleeding out on the floor.
Cops run up and take guns.
Colonial cops kill babies.
Politicians speak openly about loathing niggas.
In the colony Jefferson City offers no apologies.
They just ask for more colonial cops.
Needed resources from Johannesburg to
Jennings are restricted by the imperialist.

City politicians talking unity, but I ain't impressed
with your white savior complexes.

Black alderman with a grip on all the sexist sins.
Couldn't come together once
to fight the colonialists.

These are just some thoughts as
I chill out at the pub, the brewery,
the bar.
Put some change in the machine,
play some Jay, some Future, some Nas.

Run Don't Look Back Just Run

He's got a gun to my head. The barrel spirals like dirty water swirling down a drain. Memories, like clear water, swirling down the dark drain of my thoughts focused on this gun barrel which is dark as the night's purple sky.

Dark as daddies dreams of jungle warfare. It was dark as the apparel I was in. Wearing a brown jacket, blue jeans and my favorite pare of caramel casual shoes. Shoes that were supposed to be propped up on a chair at a bar while a friend performed awe-inspiring acoustic music. Another friend was picking me up.

I left the house for a second to get fresh air. Night air fresher than newly bloomed hyacinths. I waited leaning against my broke down inky Camry coup in front of my pale garage, which was next to a shadowed alley dotted with tarnished street lights. Barely illuminating streets cold and black as the 9mm my homeboy held below his belly. In Megiddo while he's driving he tells me,

You ready?

He's on some 'I'm a beat a niggas ass for fucking with my sister shit.' I'm like yeah, in the vermillion Monti Carlo. It's a nebulous night, my feet are blistered, it's just nice to sit down, rest my head in the oyster chair, hunched over like Stephen Hawking. Thinking about the job is like spiders crawling up my back. Spent the day at the gym cleaning upper income people's sweat off treadmills.

Standing for hours, bending my knees, stressing out because my boss is a hardcore cynic, a splinter, a hang nail on the worlds pinky toe. Open a mini bottle of Jack Daniels, guzzle it as I'm staring at old abandoned buildings he's passing. I'm slightly relaxed.

I didn't know what my home boy was gonna do when he found that nigga, But I know he was thinking of all the awful things. Imagining unlawful scenes as he muttered in audibly. Because family is important. It's important to deal with the drama so it doesn't stress out his grandma who was tired, feet and back hurting from working.

He wants to attack that man with copper fists punching through flesh like that abuser was a paper target flailing in the wind at the range. When we turned the corner past a peppery pasty church, we saw him creeping down the cracked-up sidewalk. Our eyes were glued to him in a bloodless tee shirt. When he turned his head, veered his eyes back in our direction he jetted down a street and disappeared.

My homeboy's phone rang. He got a call from his sister. She's like kill the search, like she's watching, probably perched on some branch. Like some kind of angel thinking she could save that dude. Or thinking she loved him. Or thinking she could trust him not to do it again. She forgave him. He snuck around us. Around red brick houses and apologized, probably insincerely, shallow and pedantic. This confuses me, because of how I dramatize my own mistreatment.

That leaves me psychologically traumatized. Because
I see what a shitty man can do through my momma's
eyes. Before she met my daddy another man left her
with four sons. In a large white house. For at least one
of her sons his father died. Sometimes their father
skulks around that white house.

I'm thinking why did his sister listen when that nigga
apologized? As I sent glances at streetlights that shined,
dimly on-scarred weather worn sidewalks, which were
cold as ice in the Antarctic. Cold as my mother's hospital
room floor. Sidewalks barely warmed by the steps of
people who haunt tenebrous streets and street corners.

One of these people a drifter, in a somber sooty hoody
and baggy sweat pants, was moving quickly down the
side walk. Several other specters were standing in the
alley next to the garage. It seemed as if they were
poltergeists in my periphery that came out of nowhere.
The drifter looked at me with eyes that said he had been
smoking marijuana since he woke up. With eyes dark as
the night's purple sky. He asked me as shifty as a viper

You got a lighter?

One hand was still in his pocket. I let him borrow my
lighter. I pull it out and it glimmered in the street lights
bright as my nieces smile when she sees her mother
entering the front door. He pulled out a small black pistol.
It was two feet from my head. My attention whirlpooled
into the barrel. All I saw was the barrel. Black as a black
hole. Bottomless, except for the bullet in the chamber.
He states, imperatively

Empty them pockets.

I look at him, shakily and anxious as a child
before a beating, saying,

OK
I reach into every pocket and pull out my phone, my
MP3 player, my pens. When I finish, standing in front
of my car a shell of a person, I ask him.

What else?

Then he tells me,

Run, don't look back just run.

But the problem is he's got a gun to my head. The barrel
spirals like dirty water swirling down a drain. Memories,
like clear water, swirling down the dark drain of my
thoughts. Looking down the barrel I think about the last
time I saw my niece. My sister was dropping her off at
school. Looking down the barrel, I see my father telling
my niece,

Grand-daddy love you but you need to be quiet.

Looking down the gun barrel I could see the darkness.
It was dark as when Mike went to prison. It was dark as
when momma was in the hospital. He's got a gun to my
head. Memories swirling down the dark drain of my
thoughts focused on this gun.

Having This Gift is Like Having a Gun

He, in a blue coat, asked me if it made me feel safe.

I told him that,

Having this gift is like having a gun.
You just wanna use it on somebody.

Pull it out,
stick it in somebody's scalp
and open their minds.

Is what I told him walking the streets of Paris.
Next to the emerald Sin.
Over an antediluvian bridge.
Bridging the gap in our semantic lens.
Understanding that

Having this gift is like having a gun.
You just wanna use it on somebody.

Pull it out,
stick it in somebody's scalp
and open their minds.

Is what I told him walking the streets of Paris.

Next to the emerald Sin.
He said this sentiment surprised him.
Shocked him,
like 1000 volts to the chakra below his spine.

It's not worth your life.
This destructive convention of masculinity.

I responded,

Having this gift is like having a gun.
You just wanna use it on somebody.

Pull it out,
stick it in somebody's scalp
and open their minds.

Phone Rings

Walking, stalking, talking to these streets. Houses square like cardboard boxes in patterns that repeat. Cops Stalking, but rarely. Talking to a dude who just got out of jail, Now he's free but barely. See a kid on a bike riding it care free as an old lady sitting a yard chair leans back into reflection.

Phone rings.
She's at work, she can't answer.
Phone rings.
She missed the call.
She calls back
An digital voice claims the number is disconnected.
Phone rings.
Picked it up they said they got him. Her son's too young for school. Never been told to empty them pockets. Empty them pockets is what they told her. Trade her partner for the cash and the weed.

She did taxes in the hood for people who worked long hours. Some thugs jealous and sour wanted a piece. She did taxes, for mothers smothered in kids, little bad ass bums. They went to her for a tax refund

She had to deal with the unappreciative. The gutter, the greediest of the proletariat. Dealing with people intentionally coming short with money, but she was on them religiously.

Waiting outside homes. For her this is pursuing a goal inconspicuously. When she caught you, ain't no cop out, she's like a cop out on a steak out hunting these vampires with the steak out but when they paid she bought weed stored it, sold it. Weed green as cash. She smoked it. Some thugs jealous and sour wanted a piece. One cat, who owed money for child support, received less than he thought he would. The debts he ignored came back to hunt him. So he and some cohorts, his cousin's, hatched a plan to kidnap a tax preparer.

It was her partner. They would see him walking. Flaunting the green. He had some yams he wanted all to see. They kicked in the door, the dude looked down a telescope barrel. He was rushed in to a car.
A spectral vision of peril. They all had something to prove. One sought to be a peacock. Another sought that peacock with his peeps glock.

The antagonist called her up.
Phone rings.
Picked it up, they said they got him. Got to get all the weed, the cash, everything. All her work. Time to wake up from that dream, because of this dumb nigga. Always trying to be flashy. Always in new shit, new jeans, like some amateur new on the scene.
She rushed to a gas station up the street

Here yo shit, nigga, let him go!

The antagonist stands outside the vehicle yelling something incoherent waving a pistol, pants sagging.

I ain't afraid of no gun, let him go!

She yelled defiantly, thinking, what's this bitch ass nigga saying. Not really giving a shit.
Stress pushed her apathy to the forefront. Almost not caring if he lived, but she came to far. She wanted a blunt, but it was gone, she felt no love. All her hard work, all she was saving. Tossed the green on the pavement,

Let's make the fucking trade, shit!

They wanted more, but she said,

Let him go!

Let my nigga go!

A cop appeared, but she already emptied her pockets. Came around not to long after they released her partner. She got him. Put his ass in the car and as she drove away. She noticed the cop speaking casually to the kidnappers.

The fucking cops were in on it!

Phone rings again.

Disagreements Among Friends

*How you gonna disagree on facts when science
has given us no proof of this?
Even Houdini made a career out of disproving this shit.*

My friend responded,

*Ok, whatever you can win that. Now tell me
what's really going on?*

In Iva's apartment the windows were as open as her opinions, with flies and other polychromatic flying critters crawling on the white kitchen table, relaxed with a look that said,

Fuck your feelings of disgust.

As the day turns to night, the spinach green leaves of that wooden behemoth, the tree outside the window, becomes as dark as the paranormal video Iva was playing on her iPhone.

The camera captured a room in an office building. The image was filtered through that translucent green that can only be seen in night vision settings. The leather chairs moved on their own. The metallic file cabinets opened only to spew papers, like a spring of off-white rectangles streaming into the office ether.

My response was,

This is a set up. Either somebody got fired or this 9/11 inside job was a joke.

Iva said,

I don't know, it looks like it could be real.

She spoke with a seriousness, like her words were in suits in a Chicago financial firm.
Now this is when I had the thought

*How you gonna disagree on fact when science
has given us no proof of this?
Even Houdini made a career out of disproving this shit.*

But these explanations were only a cover for my true feelings. Feeling sharp and void in my other friends' basement starring at the row of russet shark teeth on a wall adjacent to me.
My friend said,

Now tell me what's really going on?

I believed that friends should agree on everything, but especially facts. I came to his basement to chill out and talk about things we agree on. I came to his basement to reinforce my cognitive dissonance. To reinforce my world view, because I constantly question my self-worth.
I felt like if friends can't agree on everything then how are we friends?

Physicians and Philologists

We must be physicians and philologists
anti-apologists.
At bottom woman is a serpent.
Because of her we have science.
Because of her
we learned to question
that idiot man,
that patriarchal specimen.
His mind harkens back
to the labyrinth.
The dark recesses.
While we the physicians and philologists
live among symbols.
Reality is symbols.
We dance to a reality of symbols.

Talking to My Dad

Before I got into my car, my dad, with one hand on his oak cane, dressed in a dark blue mechanic's outfit, asked me,

How's the girlfriend?

I was usually in a bit of a rush reconnecting a terminal to my car battery, but I responded,

She is fine.

I used to huff and puff like Thomas the Train failing to go off the rails in a futile attempt to avoid a massive sinkhole as the tracks are going vertically down into the darkness, an iron water fall. That pit was the abyss of questions I couldn't answer. The pit became a tunnel. I used to pop my head onto the surface on occasion when his questions and demands became to muggy.

On one such occasion a few years back my dad asked me to drive him to Family Dollar.It was a sweltering day with a pale sapphire sky, but I had to take a massive dump. I don't remember what he had to get, but I do remember that I had diarrhea so I was in a hurry to leave the store.We weren't in the store particularly long. As we left briskly through the crystal portal we ran into a Jehovah's Witness. We knew it was one of them because of what he wore — a black suit sharper than a ceramic blade. He was clasping a flyer with the iconic *Watchtower* on it, in one hand. When this man opened his mouth releasing words with expelling libretto like a geyser of propaganda saying,

Excuse me, have you heard the good news? Have you heard the word? I would like to talk to you.....

My father, a Baptist preacher who refers to many non-Christians as devil people, demonic, etc, interrupted with,

We worship Jesus. We don't do nothing else.

Oh, I worship Jesus too,"

said the forlorn converter, who didn't have a chance in hell at this point or any other.

No you don't,

inserted my father, growing irritated.

He was as irritated as when he was in the indomalaya ecozone where ebony, teak, palm, mangroves, and bamboo grow with very viridian evergreens, where juvenile mantis's prey, a white soldier, uncomfortable in his whiteness, called him nigger. He felt like several assassin ants crawled up his back then ripped into his skin, only to eat their way out like a reversal of Ridley Scott's Alien. His rage was a boiling gasoline soup heated by an overheated propane tank careening in to the sums corona. He was pissed like when that one nigga said he

was gonna kill his family. You don't ever say that shit to
my daddy. His feet pressed in on the jungle floor on sticks,
piss, bullet shells and earth. It's the loneliness of existing
black overseas in a lake of white in an ocean of green.
He always took care of himself, his family, his dignity.
He used to fuck niggas up in St. Louis. See he only knew
how to protect, react and dissect faces with fists.He lifted
his bister fawn fists ready to drop that cracker like a
howitzer shell. Until someone grabbed his arm, his soul,
heart and told him

He ain't worth it.

Daddy cooled and considered those words.
This battle won't be won in a fist fight. He had to learn
how to depend on his friends. He had to depend on God
for strength. But when you get Daddy started on the
subject of Jesus he will spill information like a busted oil
tanker in the Gulf of Mexico.
I had to be the one to tell Daddy,

This ain't worth either one of yalls time!

Because neither the Jehovah's witness or my father was
willing to give ground. The back-and-forth went on for
another minute and a half before I said,

*You aren't gonna agree with him and he isn't gonna agree
with you and I have to poop. Can we go?*

I was frustrated, because the tunnel was also his hedge of
control. But when the need raised its irritated head
I broke out.

Now I'm content in that moment when he asks me,

How's the girl?

I didn't want to give him the time because I believed that we had nothing in common. When he left the house to go to work I enjoyed it. Sometimes I wonder if I enjoyed him more when he was not home. But now I respect him for giving me the space to be my own person and develop in to someone people could respect.

He then asks,

When we gonna meet her?

I say,

At some point?

But I don't think they will ever meet. As nice as it feels giving him this moment, which is the least I can do for the man who laid the ground work that is me, I only want positive reviews from him. Not those talks we used to have about my x's. Those talks used to make me feel like I was being stuffed in a box and shipped to an island of anxiety, which is always cloudy and full of serpents of apprehension that will slither up your pants leg and around your back like a league of German cock roaches.

Now I cherish my time with him, every chance I get.

$5.00 is too much for one noodle.

That morning before I left I kissed her, she was extremely tired sitting on the couch. Prostrate and sleepy. At the hospital she was laying on her side as we prayed for her. The breathing machine was pumping air in her lungs. Lungs full of fluids. She took me to another place because I was too weak to help her with her burden.

She took me with her to a restaurant where she was seated. Sitting in the cherry golden interior of the Chinese restaurant, enjoying the soup she ordered, she was surprised by her brother's desire to simply walk out without paying.

$5.00 is too much for one noodle.
Said her brother.

He told her to go outside and he'll go to the bathroom then he will meet her outside take her hand and they will run so it with look cute like a sibbling version of Bonnie and Clyde. But it wouldn't be cute. It's wrong. Seattle certainly wasn't the worst place for blacks in the mid-70s, but there was no truly good place for blacks anywhere, the prospect of being caught scared her, and not to mention the fact that they were screwing over a reputable business. But none of this mattered as he started gesturing for her to leave.

But this 'is' stealing.

She stated this very impatiently, because the guilt
weighed heavy on her. She knew that it was stealing.
Good church women, good mothers, good people, don't
steal. Her brother was used to cheating people, he used
to steal cheese and sell it at inflated prices. He was the
type of negro that would push an old lady over at the
bank if she asked him,

Could you help me check my balance?

No it's not we are just walking away.

What if we get caught?
She asked.

We won't. I did this last week.

A doctor crept into the make shift room and reported
what we already knew.

Fluids backed up in her legs.

But she was breathing, pushing boulders, surviving.
Her kidneys just need a little help. Because when the
kidneys can't process fluids effectively then fluids get
backed up into the lungs. Fluid boulders slipping past
the kidneys. But her mother faced down white
degenerates. Her father faced down Nazi armies.
Her uncle faced down overseers. So she could face this.
She put her hands together, NO, we put our hands
together creating tiny buckets, dumping fluids
out of her lungs.

Somnambulist

The city got me trapped in somnambulism.
Gods buried children alive.
That's why I had to have the schism
from a rigid idealism to pragmatism.

Pragmatics of my drastic dogmatism transcends
fanaticism.

I lost religion after I witnessed
Paul Ryans privileged privatize twin barrels
drive by Ms Daisy, with Fitzgerald driving drunk.

So I dove into literature.
Got a literary pictionary,
literally speaking daggers.

Causing primitive patriarchs to Shakespeares
Like a Zulu army horrified after watching Macbeth
actresses massacred by a maglev into platters,
let's fast track.
Turning my brand of urban semiotics
into speech acts.

Stygian Street

I was driving down the stygian street. The street was barely lit up by my headlights, but to my left, beneath the luminous street lights, I could see the dark greenery leaning out of the black gate that guarded the cemetery. The tallest grave stones could be seen jutting out of a steep viridian hill. The grave stones were like silver towers standing ominously in the darkness.
To my right there were drab warehouses of a dark umber color with light emanating from several windows.

Driving down the pummeled street I noticed a white car; it was an Impala. I could see the siren atop the vehicle, it was absent any florescence. But it's something you never fail to recognize while driving at night.
In the day time, they can be seen them parked on the side of the road. Some people slow down to see if the vehicle is occupied. Often they are not.

They exist as warnings.

Warnings my sister was trying to heed while driving the stygian street. Her feet were blistered, her legs tense as Mike Pence in a gay pride parade. Seemed like she'd been driving since the ice age to Texas for a new job.
She had a little something to smoke earlier, some weed, to take the edge off.

I imagined the flashing red and blue headlights that she must have seen. With the police car behind me, I gripped and grappled the steering wheel, trying to tear it off the fucking car because the police officer is following me for no reason.

Following her for no reason during the sunny day. Sunny as a solar flare sun bathing in the Sahara. Warm as hot coffee water boarded in a pot of boiling water. Sister was boiling pissed as a drunk old man with no more strength in his blather. She pulled the car off to the side of the road saying,

SHIT!

She said,

SHIT

at a level that was high, but not high enough for the officer to hear. The officer got out of hit vehicle one foot at time. Time waited on his steps. Time waited on his stride to her vehicle. Time started to progress when he started speaking. But for me it was still night on the stygian street. Time froze as I wondered

Why are you following me? I ain't did shit!

She ain't did shit! But it was time for her to move. She knew it wasn't time for her to be treated like the American citizen she was, but she didn't know that it was time for her to be assaulted. Head on the side of the car, shit escalated. The officer was angry as a bull. Which must be why he hit her with so much bullshit. He was on her back with her prone on the filthy side of the street claiming that she resisted arrest.

We talk about our brothers getting killed but we forget that our sisters can get it to. I got sisters who have dodged bullets like Neo while waiting in a Burger King drive thru beneath a nebulous sky.

Sisters beating niggas asses for brutally beating sisters.
Sisters anointing sisters,
sisters loving sisters.

Time started to progress when I looked for escape down shadowed streets I passed. I looked for escape from the feeling, from the fear, from the possibility that I will be pulled over, asked for my license and registration, and shot for doing something I was asked to do.

It felt like the cemetery was beckoning me, inviting me to crash into that gate if I needed to avoid the officer. But I looked at the light emanating from a warehouse window and the police car passed me.

Brand Nubian

Introducing
Brand Nubian Nirvana
sipping, guzzling Stag.
Trying to drown out trauma.
Stationary as a vacant stare he's
been placed there by feet weary
from chasing nightmares.

I came here for convivial diverting enjoyment.

I'm trying to stop whining and stop lying.
Too much to be proud of.
New young musicians singing.
Fuck the bullshit,
this towns a musical melting pot.
Individuals mixing,
moving to new music.
Young physicians selling pot.
Me and my cousins went to his crib
Bumping,
blasting bombastic beautiful sexist tunes.
Went back to their crib.
Making music with them
where music lives.
Music vivid as livid

Christians preaching
from pulpits on street corners.
They bought some weed and drove
from Ferguson to Berkeley.
The night was caliginous
as prosecutorial sentences.
Thinking about these police, hurting free
beings on the border
of being and not being.
In their small white house
the beat was dropped,
like youthful fantasies of thick models.
Dropping assets,
like criminals fleeing a trap house,
the beat was an auditory light house.

I came here for convivial diverting enjoyment.

Employing this ecstasy,
this hash to repress me as I relax chatting.
Thinking about the party at the apartment I'm in.
I raid the fridge and stoke my fire with the
depressant, beer.
They had the reefer out,
I brought the liquor we were loud.

RC Patterson is a St. Louis resident. He attained a master's in Philosophy from the University of Missouri St. Louis. RC Patterson is an Adjunct professor at Harris-Stowe State University. He has six published books including, *Black Lives Splatter, Jim CroMagnon Man,* and *Elegies.* He is an artist, a writer and a teacher.

This project was made possible, in part, by generous support from the Osage Arts Community.

Osage Arts Community provides temporary time, space and support for the creation of new artistic works in a retreat format, serving creative people of all kinds — visual artists, composers, poets, fiction and nonfiction writers. Located on a 152-acre farm in an isolated rural mountainside setting in Central Missouri and bordered by ¾ of a mile of the Gasconade River, OAC provides residencies to those working alone, as well as welcoming collaborative teams, offering living space and workspace in a country environment to emerging and mid-career artists. For more information, visit us at www.osageac.org

www.ingramcontent.com/pod-product-compliance
Lightning Source LLC
Chambersburg PA
CBHW030132100526
44591CB00009B/613